TIM VICARY

The Mysterious Death of
Charles Bravo

OXFORD UNIVERSITY PRESS

OXFORD
UNIVERSITY PRESS

Great Clarendon Street, Oxford OX2 6DP

Oxford University Press is a department of the University of Oxford.
It furthers the University's objective of excellence in research, scholarship,
and education by publishing worldwide in

Oxford New York

Auckland Cape Town Dar es Salaam Hong Kong Karachi
Kuala Lumpur Madrid Melbourne Mexico City Nairobi
New Delhi Shanghai Taipei Toronto

With offices in

Argentina Austria Brazil Chile Czech Republic France Greece
Guatemala Hungary Italy Japan Poland Portugal Singapore
South Korea Switzerland Thailand Turkey Ukraine Vietnam

OXFORD and OXFORD ENGLISH are registered trade marks of
Oxford University Press in the UK and in certain other countries

ISBN: 978 0 19 479387 2

A complete recording of this Bookworms edition of
The Mysterious Death of Charles Bravo is available in an audio CD pack. ISBN: 978 0 19 479385 8

Printed in China

Word count (main text): 11,550

For more information on the Oxford Bookworms Library,
visit www.oup.com/elt/bookworms

ACKNOWLEDGEMENTS

Illustrations by: Adam Willis/Artist Partners

The publishers would like to thank the following for permission to reproduce images: Getty Images
pp.12 (Bravo inquest/Hulton Archive), 14 (Florence Bravo/Hulton Archive), 27 (Dr James Gully/
Hulton Archive), 41 (The Priory, Balham/Hulton Archive), 51 (Charles Bravo/Hulton Archive);
John Frost Historical Newspapers pp.10 (Four Doctors), 13 (Charles Bravo & Florence Ricardo)

CONTENTS

PEOPLE IN THIS STORY

Florence Bravo, *wife of Charles Bravo;*
previously, Florence Ricardo, wife of Alexander Ricardo
Charles Bravo, *second husband of Florence Bravo;*
died April 1876
Joseph Bravo, *stepfather of Charles Bravo*
Alexander Ricardo, *first husband of Florence Bravo;*
died April 1871
Dr James Gully, *famous doctor, and lover of Florence Bravo*
Mrs Jane Cox, *friend and companion of Florence Bravo*
George Griffiths, *Florence Bravo's coachman*
Mary Ann Keeber, *Florence Bravo's maidservant*

Doctors who saw Charles Bravo during his illness:

Dr Harrison, *a doctor from Streatham*
Dr Moore, *a doctor from Balham*
Dr Royes Bell, *a doctor and cousin to Charles Bravo*
Dr George Johnson, *a well-known London doctor, and a*
friend of Royes Bell
Dr William Gull, *doctor to Queen Victoria, and the most*
famous doctor in England at that time

THE MYSTERIOUS DEATH
OF CHARLES BRAVO

In England in the 1800s, during the time of Queen Victoria, women did not have an easy time. A married woman had to obey her husband in everything; she could not decide things for herself. Only a man could do that for her. And if she had a bad husband, who beat her, she could do nothing about it.

Florence Bravo was young, beautiful, and rich, but she was not lucky in her husbands. Her first husband drank too much, and beat her. She left him and took a lover, who was kind and gentle, but he was already married. Then she married Charles Bravo . . .

Five months later, Charles Bravo was dead, killed by antimony poisoning. But who gave him the antimony? Who wanted him dead? Or was it an accident, and not murder at all?

This is a true story about a murder in 1876. It was a very famous case. The newspapers at the time were full of it, and everybody in England was talking about it. But no murderer was ever found . . .

OXFORD BOOKWORMS LIBRARY
True Stories

The Mysterious Death of Charles Bravo

Stage 3 (1000 headwords)

Series Editor: Jennifer Bassett
Founder Editor: Tricia Hedge
Activities Editors: Jennifer Bassett and Christine Lindop

Chapter 1

A true story

THIS is a true story. But although it is true, no one knows exactly what happened. That's why it is so interesting.

On Friday 21st April 1876 a young lawyer, Charles Bravo, died at his home in Balham, which at that time was a village just south of London.

But why did Charles Bravo die? Did he kill himself? Was he murdered? Or was his death just a terrible accident?

At first, the doctors thought Mr Bravo had killed himself. But then his family started asking questions. 'I met him on Tuesday afternoon,' said his cousin, Dr Royes Bell. 'He was healthy and happy then. I want to know what happened.'

'I'm sure Charles didn't kill himself,' said his stepfather, Joseph Bravo. 'He was a strong, brave young man. I think he was murdered.'

Charles Bravo was killed by a poison, antimony. But how did the poison get into his body? Did he take it himself, or did someone give it to him? If so, how? And where did the antimony come from?

During July and August 1876, the London Coroner held

an enquiry to answer these questions. At the enquiry, the police told their story, and so did Charles Bravo's friends, and the servants in his house. Famous lawyers asked questions. All over England, people read the story in their morning newspapers.

'Who killed Charles Bravo?' they asked. 'Or did he kill himself?'

The longest newspaper stories were about three people: Charles's wife, Florence; Florence's friend, Jane Cox; and Florence's lover, Dr James Gully.

These three people told their stories, but there are differences between the stories. So were they all telling the truth – or only some of the truth? And if one of them told a few lies, which one was it? And why did he or she lie?

What really happened to Charles Bravo?

Here are the three most important stories. First, Charles's wife, Florence . . .

Chapter 2

Florence Bravo's story

PART 1

My name is Mrs Florence Bravo. I am 31 years old. I live at The Priory, in Balham. At the time of his death, my husband, Charles Bravo, lived there too. My friend and companion, Jane Cox, was also living in the house . . .

My husband Charles and I were very happy together. Of course, we argued sometimes, but that's normal, isn't it? All husbands and wives argue sometimes. But Charles was a good man – a lawyer – and I loved him very much. He loved me too – everyone will tell you that. In fact, that was the last thing he said, before he died. 'You've been the very best of wives, Florence,' he said. Then I kissed him, and he died.

Charles Bravo was my second husband. I married him at the end of last year, December 1875. My first husband, Alexander Ricardo, died in 1871. I was only nineteen when I married Alexander. He was a soldier in the British army. He looked very tall and handsome in his red coat.

Both our families were very rich, and my parents liked him. All the most important people in London came to our wedding – it was wonderful! We danced late into the night.

He was the most beautiful man I had ever seen. I fell in love with him, and I thought he loved me too.

But I was wrong. Alexander was a terrible husband.

Florence Ricardo – later, Florence Bravo

He didn't love me; he spent most of his time visiting girls and drinking. He drank two or three bottles of wine every night. Sometimes, when he came home, he couldn't stand up. And when I argued with him, he hit me.

That's right – my tall beautiful soldier husband hit me! One day he hit me hard, in the face, three times. Then he laughed.

I left him then and ran home, to my parents. 'I can't live with this man,' I told them. 'He's stupid and dangerous. I don't want to be married any more!'

'But Alexander is your husband,' my father said. 'A wife can't leave her husband. It's against the law. You must go back to him and do what he says.'

'No!' I screamed. 'I can't, I won't! You don't understand! I don't want to see him again, ever! I wish he was dead!'

I cried so much that my parents thought I was ill. So my mother took me to a doctor, Dr James Gully.

I'll never forget that day. We arrived at Dr Gully's hospital in Malvern after a long journey. I was very tired, frightened, and unhappy. Dr Gully was a man, of course. But he didn't shout at me, like my father and my husband. He just looked at me, and listened. He was quiet and friendly and kind. In fact, I thought he was the kindest man I had ever met.

He was the only man who really liked me and understood me. But after a while, I saw that it was more than that. Dr Gully didn't just like me and understand me. He fell in love with me, too.

He can tell you about that.

Chapter 3

Dr James Gully's story

PART 1

My name is Dr James Gully. I am 68 years old. I live at Orwell Lodge, in Balham. In January 1871 I was living in Malvern, near Wales. That's where I first met Florence – Florence Ricardo, as she was called then . . .

I remember the day when I first met Florence. It was a cold January morning. There was snow on the hills, but the sun was shining. Florence's mother brought her to my hospital in Malvern. Florence was not ill, but she was very unhappy. She had run away from her husband, Alexander Ricardo. Her father had told her to go back to him.

'But I won't go!' she said. 'I'm never going back to him, never!'

I looked at her carefully. She was crying, and there was a dark bruise on her face. She was a young woman, twenty-five years old, and she had been married for six years.

'Does your husband hit you, my dear?' I asked.

'Yes, he does. He often hits me. I hate him!'

'But you're his wife, Florence,' her mother said. 'So you have to live with him. That's what wives do.'

'No!' Florence screamed at her mother. 'You don't

Dr James Gully

understand. When he's drunk, he's dangerous, he hurts me! I'll kill myself if you make me go back!'

She got up and hit her hand against the window.

'This young woman is ill,' I told her mother. 'She needs a quiet, safe place where she can rest and be calm. We have a small house in the hospital gardens. She can stay there until she is better.'

So Florence stayed, and I visited her every day. We walked in the hospital gardens, and she told me about her husband, Alexander.

'I was just a young girl when I married him,' she said. 'I didn't understand anything. It doesn't matter what a man looks like – what matters is how he behaves.'

'And how does Alexander behave?' I asked.

'Well, he left the army after we married,' she said. 'And that made him unhappy. He doesn't know what to do all day. We live in a big country house – Gatcombe Park – but he is always in London with his friends. He sees other women too, I think. When he comes home, he drinks. Two or three bottles of wine every day.'

'Don't you try to stop him?' I asked.

'Of course I do. I try. Once or twice I've put a little antimony in his wine, to make it taste bad. It made him sick, but he didn't stop drinking.'

I'd heard of this before. Antimony is a dangerous poison – it can kill you, if you take a lot. But some wives put a little of it in their husband's wine. It makes the man feel sick, so he doesn't drink so much. Some men do that to their wives, too. I think it's a bad idea.

There were tears in her eyes. 'When he's drunk, he hits me. Don't send me back to him, Dr Gully! Please don't send me back!'

'Of course I won't, my dear,' I said quietly. 'Don't worry. No woman should live with a man like that.'

But Florence was afraid that her husband Alexander would make her come home. At that time, there were very strong laws about how women must behave. Most men liked these laws, but I didn't. I thought the law was unfair to women. The law said that a married woman couldn't decide things for herself. She needed a man – a guardian – to decide things for her. Usually, this guardian was her husband or her father. But sometimes a friend could become a woman's guardian.

'If you want to leave your husband,' I said, 'I will help you. In law, I can become your guardian. I will tell my lawyers to start preparing the necessary papers now. Then your husband cannot order you to go home. And your father cannot tell you what to do either. Would you like that? Will that make you feel safe?'

'Oh yes, please, Dr Gully,' she said. 'Will you do that for me? Can you write to your lawyers today?'

I smiled. 'It will be a pleasure, my dear.'

My lawyers began work immediately. Florence's husband, Alexander, was very angry, but he could not stop me.

Florence continued to live in Malvern, and I talked to her every day. She was a beautiful, intelligent young woman, and she liked my hospital. My hospital was different to other hospitals. I gave sick people baths of cold and hot water, good healthy food, rest and quiet – and it worked! I told her about the famous people who visited me – Charles Darwin, Charles Dickens, Florence Nightingale. She liked stories like that. As time passed she began to look healthier. She began to talk happily. Sometimes she even smiled.

She had a beautiful smile. In fact she was a very beautiful young woman. The most beautiful, interesting young woman I have ever met.

I told her about my family. I was sixty-three years old then. I had a son who was ten years older than Florence, and a small granddaughter. But my wife lived in a hospital in Yorkshire. She was eighty years old, and her mind had gone; she didn't recognize me or my son. So really, I didn't have a wife any more.

When my lawyers finished their work, Florence became separated in law from her husband Alexander Ricardo, and I became her guardian.

'Can I go on living here?' she asked me.

'You can stay here as long as you like,' I said. 'But you're a free woman now. I won't tell you what to do.'

She laughed, and took my hand. 'Oh yes, James, of course. You're so kind. I'm so grateful to you.'

That was the first time she called me James, and it felt – *wonderful!* I wanted to take her in my arms and dance! Of course I didn't – she was only twenty-five, and I was sixty-three, but . . . a man can still fall in love, even when he is old.

And love hurts when you are old, just as much as it does when you are young. More, perhaps, because when you are old you have so little time left.

I wanted to take her in my arms and dance.

In April 1871 Alexander Ricardo died. He had already been ill, and after Florence left him, he drank more and more every day, and was often sick. In the end alcohol destroyed his stomach.

When he died, Florence, his widow, became a very rich lady. All her husband's money was hers. But her father wasn't her guardian. I was. Later that year, she came on holiday with me to Germany.

It was the most wonderful holiday of my life. We stayed in a town called Kissingen, in Bavaria. We walked in the hills and gardens, looking at the beautiful clean rivers. We went to restaurants and the theatre, two happy people together.

We lived together like husband and wife. In fact, some people in the hotel thought she *was* my wife. We laughed and talked all day. I'm sure it was easy to see that I was in love with her.

I couldn't stop looking at her and thinking about her. Everything I did, everything I thought or wrote or said, was for her.

So what about her? Was she in love with me?

I thought she was. She looked wonderful, she laughed and sang as we walked through the town together. We danced for hours in the evening; she was strong and healthy – stronger than me. She talked to me all the time, she called me 'her famous doctor'. I thought she was happy to be with me, to spend all day and all night together.

Isn't that love?

Chapter 4

Florence Bravo's story

PART 2

My name is Mrs Florence Bravo. I am 31 years old. I live at The Priory, in Balham. At the time of his death, my husband, Charles Bravo, lived there too. My friend and companion, Jane Cox, was also living in the house . . .

I liked Dr Gully a lot. He was the most intelligent man I had ever met. He told me interesting things, and he made me laugh. He was also very kind – much kinder than my husband Alexander, or my father.

I was very happy on that holiday in Germany. We went everywhere together; we talked and laughed all day, and sang and danced in the evening. For a short time, I thought I was in love with him. But of course he was much, much older than me. Some people in the hotel thought he was my grandfather. Some of them smiled at us, but others looked at us angrily. We slept together in the same bedroom, but we were not married. Most people thought that was very wrong.

One evening, he asked me to marry him. I was surprised. It was impossible, of course. I didn't know what to say. I smiled and touched his face.

'James, that's a lovely idea,' I said. 'But we can't marry, can we? You have a wife.'

'Yes, I know,' he said. 'But she's old and ill; she won't live long. Will you wait for me, Florence? Please? We can marry when she's dead.'

I walked away from him, slowly. *I don't want to make him unhappy*, I thought, *but . . . what will people say if I marry a man more than twice as old as me?*

'It's very difficult, James,' I said. 'My parents won't talk to me because of you. They say I need a husband of my own age. Perhaps they're right. We are good friends – isn't that enough?'

He held my hands and looked into my eyes. I could see he was hurt.

'You should marry the man you love,' he said. 'That's the right thing to do. Any other kind of marriage will be a lie – a terrible mistake.'

I looked up at him. 'Yes, James, I know. Don't worry – I don't want another husband like Alexander. Let me think about this, will you? It's not easy to decide.'

———

When we came back to England, I bought a large house called The Priory. It was in a village called Balham, near London. Dr Gully left his hospital in Malvern and bought a house called Orwell Lodge, just five minutes' walk away from my house. We met nearly every day – I had a key to his house, and he had a key to mine. We went for walks and rides in the countryside around Balham. We were still friends. It was almost as good as in Germany.

The Priory, Balham – Florence Bravo's home

Almost, but not quite. I was young – I wanted friends of my own age. But I couldn't make new friends because Dr Gully was always there. People knew we weren't married, so they didn't want to know us. Often, married women walked past me in the street, with their noses in the air. They knew me very well, but they refused to speak to me or even look at me. To them, I was just something dirty in the street.

That made me miserable and angry. It was so unfair: no one was unkind to Dr Gully, because he was a man! Men – even married men – can do what they like. But if a woman does something wrong, then no one will speak to her.

I needed a woman friend – someone I could talk to about women's things, when James was not there. I put an advertisement for a 'lady companion' in a newspaper, and a woman called Jane Cox answered it.

I liked Jane. She was a widow, and she needed money to send her three children to school. So I gave her the job, and she came to live with me. We became friends. We talked, all the time, and went shopping together.

I'm not sure if Dr Gully liked Jane. He was very polite to her, but sometimes, I think, he wished she was not there. He wanted to be my only friend.

But that's why I needed Jane. I needed a woman to talk to about Dr Gully. He was kind, and clever, but he was so much older than me. I was lonely, and worried. I didn't know what to do.

And then one day I fell ill. I was in bed for several weeks. My companion, Jane Cox, looked after me. I talked to her a lot. She liked Dr Gully, but she didn't want me to marry him.

'His wife may live for ten more years,' she said. 'Anyway, you need a younger man.'

'It's easy to say that, Jane,' I said. 'But where can I find a young man who is as clever and kind as James Gully?'

'I think I know someone,' Jane said.

'Really, Jane?' I asked. 'Who?'

Jane smiled. 'I know a family called Bravo. I met them in Jamaica. They have a son called Charles. I think you'll like him.'

Chapter 5

Dr James Gully's story

PART 2

My name is Dr James Gully. I am 68 years old. I live at Orwell Lodge, in Balham. In January 1871 I was living in Malvern, near Wales. That's where I first met Florence – Florence Ricardo, as she was called then . . .

It was that man, Charles Bravo, who caused all the trouble. Everything was fine before that. I saw Florence every day, we went for walks and rides around Balham together. We were very happy. But then . . .

One day, a few weeks after Florence had been ill, I came to her house as usual. Her companion, Jane Cox, met me at the door. 'I'm sorry, Dr Gully, but Florence isn't at home.'

I was surprised, and hurt. This had never happened before. 'Where has she gone?'

'She is visiting a family called Bravo. They are businessmen and lawyers, I think, from Jamaica.'

Without me, I thought sadly. 'Well, tell her I called, will you? I hope to see her tomorrow.'

———

The next time I saw Florence, she was a different woman.

She seemed happy and excited, but worried too. She didn't look me in the eyes. I asked her to have dinner with me in the evening.

Charles Bravo

'Oh, I'm sorry, James,' she said. 'But I can't. I'm going to the theatre with someone.'

'Someone?' I asked. 'Who?'

'Charles Bravo. I met him the other day.'

'Oh, I see. What's he like, this Charles Bravo?'

She looked away from me to hide the excitement in her eyes. But there was a smile on her face – she couldn't hide that. 'Oh, very polite and friendly. He's an interesting man – a lawyer. He's quite handsome, and funny, too. You'll like him, I expect.'

I felt a sudden terrible pain in my chest. It was difficult to breathe. I *knew* – I knew then that I had lost her. 'How old is he?' I asked.

'Quite young – like me. James, are you all right?'

'It's my chest. I'll have to sit down. I'll be all right in a few minutes.'

She sat down beside me, but she didn't look at me, even then. And I wasn't all right – not in a few minutes, or a few hours or a few days. I was never all right again. I had lost her to a younger man, and there was nothing I could do to change it.

I met Charles Bravo a few weeks later. He was walking in the village with Florence on his arm – as I used to walk with her. She was right; he was handsome, and young. But he wasn't polite or friendly, not to me. He looked at me as a man looks at an enemy. He smiled coldly.

'Florence has agreed to marry me, Doctor Gully,' he said. 'She will soon be Mrs Charles Bravo.'

'Congratulations,' I said. But my voice sounded strange,

and I had that terrible pain in my chest. 'I hope you will be very happy.'

'Oh, we will, Doctor Gully, we will,' he said, with that cold smile on his face. 'I expect you were happy too, when you married your wife, all those long years ago. Is Mrs Gully well?'

From his words, from the look on his face, it was clear that Florence had told him all about me, and about the love there had been between us. All during this conversation Florence stayed close to his side and looked down at the ground. Not once did she lift her eyes to my face.

'My wife is . . . in a hospital in Yorkshire,' I said. 'She is an old, sad woman.'

'But still *alive*, I hope, Dr Gully?' he said, as I turned and walked quickly away. 'Your wife is still alive, I hope, and in good health?'

I hated him then, and I have hated him ever since. I continued to live at my house in Balham – where else could I go? – and in December 1875 I saw Florence go to her wedding with that man. She looked more beautiful than ever. She drove past my house on the way to the church. But she didn't look at me, not once. Not on her wedding day, not in all the weeks afterwards. If I passed her in the street, she looked away, or talked to her friend, Jane Cox. I felt like a dead man, a ghost.

Then one day in March I met Mrs Cox on a train to London. She asked me for some medicine for her mother in Jamaica. I promised to send it to her.

'How is Florence?' I asked. 'Is she happy?'

Jane Cox shook her head sadly. 'Not really, no. She was ill in bed last week.'

'I'm sorry to hear it,' I said. 'But what about her husband, Charles. Is he kind to her?'

'That man?' Mrs Cox said angrily. 'He doesn't know how to be kind to a woman. Everything he does makes her unhappy. She argued with him last Tuesday, and he hit her.'

'He *hit* her?' I was so angry, my hands began to shake. 'You mean, he *hit* Florence, after she had been ill?' 'Yes,' Jane Cox said. 'It's not a happy marriage, Dr Gully. He is only interested in one thing – her money.'

I was sad and very angry, but there was nothing that I could do to help. I wasn't her guardian any more. Florence had chosen to leave me, and marry Charles Bravo. If her marriage was unhappy, that was her problem, not mine. Perhaps she hated her young husband, I don't know. But I can't believe she killed him. She's too sweet, too kind, too beautiful to do anything like that.

Some people think I killed Charles Bravo, but I didn't. I'm a doctor – my job is to make people well, not to kill them. And when did I kill him? How did I kill him? It was impossible for me to do it. I never entered Florence's house after she married Charles Bravo.

Maybe he killed himself. I don't know and I don't care. The world is a better place without him.

Jane Cox was the only friend that Florence had in that house. She tried to help Florence, I think.

Maybe she can tell you what happened.

Chapter 6

Jane Cox's story

PART 1

My name is Mrs Jane Cox. I am 49 years old. I am Florence Bravo's friend and companion. At the time of Mr Bravo's death, I was living at The Priory, in Balham. I now live in my own house in Lancaster Road . . .

THE first time I met Charles Bravo was in 1869, two years after I came to England. My husband had died in 1867, in Jamaica. I had three young sons, and very little money. Charles's stepfather, Joseph Bravo, knew my husband, and he lent me some money. I met Charles at his house.

Later, I went to work for Florence Ricardo. She was a lovely young lady – very friendly, kind, and interesting. I was her companion – my job was to talk to her and help her with the servants. Soon we became friends. We talked a lot and told each other everything.

Florence liked my sons. She was sad because she didn't have any children herself. 'I've always wanted children,' she said. 'Lots of them. But I didn't have any with Alexander, and now, well . . .' She shook her head sadly. 'To have children, I need a husband. And the right man isn't easy to find, is he, Jane?'

When I first met Florence, she was a close friend of Dr Gully. I liked him – he was a good, kind man, very easy to talk to. He had lots of interesting stories about his hospital work. I told him about my life in Jamaica – he had been to Jamaica too, when he was young.

But he was too old to marry her, and his wife was still alive. So I introduced Florence to Charles Bravo.

I know, it was a big mistake, I can see that now. But I didn't know Charles very well then. I thought he was young, clever, handsome, amusing – just the right sort of husband for Florence. And she thought the same, at first.

She talked to me about him. 'I'm not really in love with him, Jane,' she said. 'Not how I was in love with Dr Gully, but . . . well . . . Charles is my own age. A young man that I can have children with. My parents will like him. Married women will invite me to their houses and talk to me again.'

'A perfect husband, then,' I said, smiling.

'Yes,' she said. 'I suppose so.'

But he wasn't perfect, of course. I know that now. So does Florence. She found out a few days after the wedding. I heard them talking in the garden.

'How many gardeners have we got, dear?' he asked her.

'Three,' she said. 'Why do you ask, Charlie?'

'Well, three is too many,' he answered. 'They don't work hard – I saw two of them smoking this morning. I'm sure we only need one.'

'Oh, but they have families, ' said Florence, surprised. 'And . . . they love the flowers.'

'Well, they can go home to their own families and flowers,' said Charles with a cold laugh. 'From now on, we'll have one gardener, not three.'

'Oh no, Charles, please . . .'

'And another thing,' her new husband continued. 'I looked in the stables this morning. We have five horses, Florence. *Five!* That's far too many. I'm going to sell three of them next week.'

'But Charles, you can't!' Florence screamed. 'Those are *my* horses, not yours – and I love them!'

'My dear Florence,' said Charles quietly. There was something about his voice – he wasn't angry or upset as I expected. In fact, he was laughing at her – he seemed to enjoy making her unhappy! 'My dear Florence, I am your husband now, haven't you noticed? Married women don't own things, they can't. So everything that used to be yours is now mine. If I want to sell the horses, I will. It's for me to decide, and you to obey.'

'*NO!*' Florence screamed. The gardeners heard her, and looked up. She was shouting at him, screaming into his face. 'Those are *my* horses and you can't sell them! I won't let you!'

'You can't stop me, woman,' he said. Then I heard a terrible sound – the sound of his hand hitting her face. Not once, but twice. She screamed and fell to the ground. I ran to help her. There was blood on her face and she was crying. I looked into the eyes of the man who had hit her – Charles Bravo, the perfect husband. The man I had introduced her to. He was smiling.

Florence screamed and fell to the ground. I ran to help her.

'Mrs Bravo has had an accident, Jane,' he said quietly. 'Please help her. She needs to wash her face. And then perhaps she will think about what I have said. Now, I am going to talk to these gardeners.'

That was how the marriage began, and that was how it went on. Almost every week there was a new argument, and almost every time he won and she lost. If she argued, he hit her, so she stopped arguing. The gardeners left and three horses were sold.

But even that wasn't enough for him. He argued with the coachman as well.

Before she met Charles Bravo, Florence's coachman, George Griffiths, used to take her and Dr Gully for long drives in the countryside. Sometimes I went with them. Florence liked George – she was interested in horses and so was he. She paid him well, and sometimes she spent hours outside in the stable yard, talking to him and watching him work with her horses.

But everything changed when she married Mr Bravo. Charles Bravo didn't really like horses – he was afraid of them. Sometimes he hit them, and then of course they ran away. That made George angry – he was kind to his horses, so they worked well for him. And George tried to argue when Charles sold three horses. Well, Charles didn't like servants to argue with him. So he decided to get rid of George Griffiths as well.

One day when George Griffiths was driving, another coach hit them. Nobody was hurt, but Charles was angry. He said George was a bad driver and it was all his fault.

The next day he came out to the stables. I was outside, in the garden, so I saw what happened. George Griffiths was putting some white powder in water for the horses.

'What's that?' Charles asked.

'Antimony, sir,' George answered. 'It's a medicine for horses. It cleans their stomachs.'

'Stop that!' Mr Bravo said. 'You can't give antimony to horses – it's a poison!'

That made George angry. He didn't think Charles Bravo knew anything about horses.

'It's all right to give them a little, sir,' he said. 'I've worked with horses for twenty years – I know what I'm doing.'

'I don't believe you. Yesterday you hit a coach and now you're trying to poison my horses!' Charles said angrily. 'That's it! I don't want you here. You can leave this job today!'

'But sir, I've got a wife and children!' George said. 'I . . .'

'That's your problem, not mine!' Mr Bravo shouted. 'Get out of this house now, and don't come back!'

So George Griffiths lost his job. But before he left, I heard him talking to the other servants in the kitchen. He threw his coat on the table angrily.

'That man Bravo isn't just bad, he's crazy!' he shouted. 'I've worked with horses for twenty years, and now this! And he hits his wife, too – we all know that!'

'Well, you'll get a better job somewhere else, won't you?' said the cook. 'I'd like to leave too.'

'You and I can leave, but his wife can't, poor woman,' George said. 'You know what? Charles Bravo will be dead in four months. You wait and see.'

That was a strange thing to say. Did George mean *he* was going to kill him, himself? Surely not. He was just angry. But then, only a few weeks later, Charles Bravo *was* dead. So did George Griffiths kill him? Is that possible?

After all, Charles Bravo was poisoned with antimony. And George kept antimony in the stables. He used it as a medicine for the horses.

I never saw George again after that day. He got a job as a coachman with another lady, twenty miles away. And he told the Coroner he threw all the antimony away, before he left.

Maybe he did, I don't know. I don't know where he kept it. I didn't go into the stable yard very often – not as often as Florence, anyway.

But Charles went there quite often. He knew where everything was, and he was interested in medicine – that's why he knew that antimony was a poison.

So maybe he took the antimony, himself. That's what I think happened. Maybe it was an accident, but I think Charles Bravo killed himself.

Chapter 7

Jane Cox's story

PART 2

My name is Mrs Jane Cox. I am 49 years old. I am Florence Bravo's friend and companion. At the time of Mr Bravo's death, I was living at The Priory, in Balham. I now live in my own house in Lancaster Road ...

Soon after her marriage, Florence became pregnant. She was happy about this, and Charles was pleased too. 'The baby will be a boy,' he said. 'We'll call him Charles Bravo the Second!'

But Florence often felt ill. And she and Charles argued all the time – about money, the servants, the horses, everything. But the worst arguments were about Dr Gully. One day, Charles opened a letter, and started shouting angrily. 'Look at this,' he said to Florence. 'It's from Dr Gully, isn't it? This is what he thinks of me!'

Florence read the letter and showed it to me. It was a horrible letter.

'*I know why you married Florence,*' the letter said. '*You don't love her. You just wanted her money, that's all.*'

'That's awful, Charles,' Florence said. 'But I don't understand. There is no name on this letter. Who wrote it?'

'You know very well who wrote it!' Charles shouted. 'Dr Gully, of course! That's his handwriting, I'm sure it is! You've been talking to him about me, haven't you? You're still in love with him, aren't you?'

'No, Charles, I'm not!' Florence said. 'I haven't spoken to Dr Gully once since we were married. Anyway, look at this letter, this is terrible handwriting. Dr Gully writes much better than this.'

Charles Bravo smiled – a cold, angry smile. 'Really? Well, let's see. He's written lots of letters to you, hasn't he, Florence? And you've kept them, because you're in love with him. Go and find them, Florence, bring them here. Then we'll see if this handwriting is the same.'

Florence's face went quite red. 'I haven't got them, Charles,' she said. 'I sent them all back to him, before we got married. And he gave me back all my letters, too – the ones I wrote to him.'

'Oh, really? Well, where are those letters? Bring them here, let me see them.'

'I can't.' Florence started to cry. 'I can't show you anyway, because I burnt them all on the fire. And I think Dr Gully burnt all my letters too. You see, I don't love him any more, Charles. That's over, it's finished. I'm never going to see Dr Gully again.'

She stopped crying and put her hand on his arm. 'That's what you should do with this letter, too. It's a horrible letter, Charles. Just burn it, forget all about it. Just as I have forgotten Dr Gully.'

'Have you really, Florence? Are you sure?'

'Yes, Charles, I'm sure.' She put her arms around him, and leaned her head against his chest. 'You're my husband now, Charles. I'm going to have your baby. So we must be kind to each other, and not argue about silly things like this.'

Very gently, she took the letter from his hand, and threw it into the fire.

Florence didn't meet Dr Gully, but I did. I met him on the train one day, on 25th March, on the way to London. I told him about my mother in Jamaica, and asked him for some medicine for her. A few days later, he wrote to me at The Priory.

I opened the letter, but Charles didn't like that. 'Let me see that, Mrs Cox,' he said, holding out his hand. 'I'm the man of this house, I should read all the letters first, you know. Who is it from?'

'It's from Dr Gully,' I said. 'It's about my mother, that's all. She's ill in Jamaica. He writes about some medicine for her.'

He took my letter and read it. There was a list of medicines inside. Then he gave it back to me. 'Well, don't write back to him,' Charles Bravo said. 'I don't want anyone in this house to write to that man.'

Two weeks later, on 6th April, I found Florence crying in her bedroom.

'What's wrong?' I asked. 'Have you and Charles been arguing again?'

'No, it's not that,' she said. 'It's worse. Call a doctor. I think I've lost the baby.'

Florence was right; she had lost her baby. She was ill, and spent two weeks in bed. I slept in her bedroom with her. Charles didn't like that. He didn't understand how difficult such things are for women. When she stayed in bed crying, that made him angry and impatient. He thought she should get up the next day. He seemed to think that a woman losing her baby was nothing important.

But I was worried, and so I was pleased when I met Dr Gully again on the train. I told him about Florence's illness, and he promised to send some medicine for her. But he didn't want to make Charles angry, so he didn't send it to The Priory. He left it at my house, in Lancaster Road, and I took it to Florence from there.

A few days later, Charles called me into his study.

'Mrs Cox,' he said. 'I have been thinking. There are too many people in this house.'

'Too many people?' I said. 'What do you mean?'

'I mean,' he said, 'that I don't need *you* in this house any more.'

'But, sir . . . I am not here to help you. I work for Mrs Bravo.'

'Mrs Bravo is my wife. *I* make the decisions in this house, and I don't want you here any more. Every time I try to talk to my wife, you are there with her. You even sleep in her bedroom. That isn't right!'

'But she's ill, sir! She's just lost her baby. She needs me – she wants me there.'

A few days later, Charles called me into his study.

'Well, *I* don't want you there. When Florence is better, I want you to leave. Do you understand? I don't need your help any more.'

This was a terrible thing for me. I needed my job to pay for my sons' school. And Florence was my friend. I was worried about her. *If I leave*, I thought, *he can hit Florence every day, and no one will know.*

As I walked out of the room, I thought: *I hate that man, Charles Bravo. I wish he were dead.*

When I told Florence, she cried. 'Jane, please don't leave me,' she said. 'I need you here to keep me safe. Promise me you won't go!'

'I don't want to leave,' I said. 'But what can we do? He's your husband – he can do what he likes.'

'I'll talk to him,' she said. She was a brave lady, Florence. She tried to make her own decisions; she didn't want to obey her husband all the time. But Charles was a dangerous, violent man.

'What if he hits you again?' I asked. ' He may hurt you badly.' I wanted to save her, but I didn't know how.

She sat up in bed. 'I won't let him, Jane,' she said. 'You and I – we must work together. We must stop that man, before he destroys both of our lives. This is *my* house, not his. He must listen to me, and learn to do what I want.'

'But he doesn't listen to women,' I said. 'He thinks we're like children, or servants. How can you change that?'

'I'll find a way, Jane,' she said quietly. 'Don't worry, I'll find a way.'

Chapter 8

Florence Bravo's story

PART 3

My name is Mrs Florence Bravo. I am 31 years old. I live at The Priory, in Balham. At the time of his death, my husband, Charles Bravo, lived there too. My friend and companion, Jane Cox, was also living in the house . . .

WHEN Jane Cox told me what Charles had said, I was very worried. Jane was very important to me. I didn't want to lose her.

On Tuesday, April 18th, I felt a little better, so I got up. It was my first day out of bed. Jane went to Worthing to look at a holiday house for us, and I went to London with Charles. In the carriage he said: 'I'm pleased Jane's gone to Worthing, Florence. We haven't been alone together for two weeks. I'll be happy when that woman is gone.'

'Please don't say that, Charles,' I said. 'Jane is my best friend.'

'She *was* your best friend, darling,' said Charles, smiling. 'Before you met me. Now I'm your best friend, aren't I?'

'Well yes,' I answered. 'But you're my husband, Charles. I need Jane, to talk about women's things. That's what I pay her for.'

'Well, she's too expensive,' Charles said. 'I spoke to her yesterday. I told her to leave at the end of the month.'

'But Charles, you can't do that!' I said. 'She needs the money to look after her children. Anyway, she works for me, not you. So she's staying, Charles. All right?'

'No!' he shouted. He held my arm hard, really hard, and it hurt. He was strong – much stronger than me – and his face was close to mine. 'You're my wife, Florence – you do what I say! Do you understand?'

I was frightened. 'Let go of my arm, Charles! People in the street are watching – what will they think?'

'I don't care,' he said. 'It's none of their business. What are you going to do – call Dr Gully?' We were driving past Dr Gully's house at the time.

'Don't be stupid, Charles,' I said. 'You know I don't talk to Dr Gully any more. I told you – you're my husband, I love you, not him!'

'Do you?' he said. He still held my arm. 'Well, kiss me then. And forget about Jane and Dr Gully.'

I was afraid, so I kissed him. Then we drove on in silence. It was a bad start to the day, but before we got to London Charles was happy again. He talked to me kindly and told funny stories. He was often like that – angry for a short time, then friendly a few minutes later. He was a difficult man, but I tried to understand him. That's what a wife has to do, isn't it? Understand her husband and love him. But I was very worried about losing Jane.

In London Charles visited his cousin, Dr Royes Bell. I went shopping. After lunch I went home and had a rest; it was my first day out of bed. Charles came home later. He was happy and excited. 'I'm going out for a ride,' he said. He went outside and called the groom.

'Get that big horse, Cremorne, ready for me, man. Quickly, now.'

'Is that a good idea, sir?' the groom asked. 'Cremorne's been a little difficult this week.'

Charles thought he knew a lot about horses but he didn't, really. He shouted angrily at the groom. 'Don't argue with me, man! Get him ready! I know how to ride my own horse, damn you!'

But an hour later he came home, shaking. His face was white and his shirt was wet with sweat. 'That horse Cremorne is dangerous!' he said. 'We'll have to sell it.'

'Why, Charles,' I asked, 'what happened?'

'The horse ran away with me. For six miles he wouldn't stop.'

'How awful! Are you hurt? Did you fall off?'

'No, thank God, I didn't. But my arms and chest hurt. He's very strong, that horse – like a wild animal!'

'Go upstairs and rest before dinner. I'm sorry you were frightened, Charles.'

He walked slowly upstairs with his hand on his chest. At the top, he looked down angrily.

'I wasn't *frightened*, Florence, don't be silly. Anyway, it's the groom's fault, not mine. He gave the horse too much food, that's all.'

Charles still looked ill at dinner that evening. Jane talked to him about the holiday house in Worthing but he

'The horse ran away with me. For six miles he wouldn't stop.'

didn't answer. He ate a lot of food and drank three glasses of wine. After dinner I was tired, so I went up to my bedroom. Jane came up a few minutes later.

My maidservant, Mary Ann, brought me a glass of wine to help me sleep. But Charles came into my bedroom and saw it. He didn't like me drinking wine in the evening. He often tried to stop me.

'You drink too much, Florence,' he said. 'I've told you before. You'll make yourself ill.'

It's true. I did sometimes feel ill after drinking wine. I was sick once or twice, I don't know why. But wine usually made me feel warm, and sleepy. I liked that.

'I'm tired, Charles,' I said. 'Leave me alone.'

Charles went out. I lay down in bed, and Jane sat beside me, reading aloud from a book. It was peaceful in my bedroom and I was very sleepy. My maid came back in.

'Do you want anything else, madam?' she asked.

'No, thank you, Mary Ann,' I said. 'Just take the dogs downstairs, will you, please?'

Mary Ann went out with my two dogs and closed the doors behind her. There are two doors to my bedroom – an outside door and an inside door – and she closed them both. I like that; it makes the room very quiet. I lay there for a minute or two, listening to Jane's voice reading to me, and then . . .

. . . I fell asleep.

I don't know what happened next. Mary Ann says that Charles called for help. But I didn't hear him. I was asleep.

Chapter 9

What the maid saw

‎

THOSE were the three important stories heard at the London Coroner's enquiry in July and August 1876 – the stories of Florence Bravo, Dr James Gully, and Mrs Jane Cox. There was truth, and perhaps also a few lies, in all the stories.

But there were also other stories heard at the enquiry in 1876. There was Florence's maidservant, for example, Mary Ann Keeber . . .

‎

Every day the maid, Mary Ann Keeber, cleaned the bedrooms at The Priory and lit fires in them to make them warm. She always put a bottle of drinking water beside Charles Bravo's bed. Later, in the evenings, she helped Charles and Florence with anything they wanted.

On the night of Tuesday 18th April, Mary Ann closed the two doors to Florence's bedroom and went downstairs with the dogs. But halfway down the stairs, one of the dogs ran back up again. As Mary Ann turned to call it, she saw Charles Bravo open his bedroom door. His face was white and he looked afraid. 'Florence! Florence!' he shouted. 'Hot water! Hot water!' Then he ran back into his room.

Charles Bravo's face was white and he looked afraid.

Mary Ann was surprised. She waited for Florence or Mrs Cox to come out and help him, but they didn't. Perhaps they hadn't heard him, she thought. So she hurried back into Florence's bedroom. Florence was in bed with her eyes closed and Jane Cox was sitting beside her. Mary Ann told Jane what had happened. 'Come quickly,' she said. 'There's something wrong with Mr Bravo!'

Jane Cox and Mary Ann went into Charles's bedroom. They saw Charles standing by an open window. His face was grey and wet with sweat. 'Help!' he cried. 'Hot water! Hot water!' He leaned out of the window and vomited onto the kitchen roof below. Then he fell to the floor.

Mrs Cox told Mary Ann to run downstairs and fetch some hot water. When Mary Ann came back, she saw Charles sitting on the floor. Mrs Cox had her hands on his chest. She was trying to help him breathe, Mary Ann thought.

'Get some mustard – hurry!' Mrs Cox said. So Mary Ann ran downstairs again. When she came back, Jane Cox told her to put the mustard into the hot water and lift Charles's feet into it.

'It's an old way to help a sick person,' Mrs Cox said. 'Rub his feet with the hot water and mustard.'

Mary Ann tried, but Charles knocked the water over and fell on the floor with his eyes closed. So then Mrs Cox gave him some mustard and hot water to drink, and sent Mary Ann downstairs again, for hot coffee. But the coffee only made him vomit again, into a bowl.

'Go and send the groom to fetch Dr Harrison,' Mrs Cox told Mary Ann. 'And then go and fetch some camphor from my room.'

So Mary Ann ran downstairs again for the groom, then upstairs to Mrs Cox's room for the camphor, but she couldn't find it. So she went into Florence's bedroom instead.

Florence was lying in bed with her eyes closed. Mary Ann shook her arm to wake her up.

'What is it?' Florence asked. 'What's the matter?'

'It's your husband, madam,' Mary Ann said. 'Come quick. He's ill.'

'What?' Florence said. 'Where is he?'

She jumped out of bed and ran into Charles's bedroom. Mary Ann followed. Charles was lying on the floor with Jane Cox sitting beside him. Florence knelt down and took his hand.

'Charlie, what's happened?' she said. 'Speak to me, darling – what's wrong?'

But he didn't answer. His eyes were closed and he looked half dead. Jane tried to get some coffee into his mouth again but it was no good. He didn't wake up.

'Have you sent for the doctor?' Florence asked.

'Yes, madam,' Mary Ann said. 'The groom has gone for Dr Harrison, in Streatham.'

Florence looked surprised and angry. 'But he lives two miles away, he'll be too late!' she said. 'Why didn't you send for Dr Moore? He lives nearer.' She ran downstairs screaming for one of the manservants. 'Get Dr Moore from Balham, as quickly as you can. Mr Bravo is very ill, he may be dying! Hurry, man, run!' Then she came back upstairs and knelt beside her husband again.

'Try to wake up, Charlie,' she said. 'Please, try. Don't leave me now.'

Chapter 10

What the doctors saw

DURING Charles Bravo's illness, he was seen by no fewer than five different doctors. And of course, the Coroner's enquiry took a great interest in what the doctors saw, and said, and thought . . .

Dr Moore was the first doctor to arrive at The Priory on the night of Tuesday 18th April. He went upstairs to Charles Bravo's bedroom. A few minutes later, Dr Harrison arrived. Jane Cox met him at the front door.

'Mr Bravo has been sick several times,' she said. 'I think he has poisoned himself with chloroform.'

Dr Harrison went upstairs to the bedroom. Dr Moore was already there. 'This man is very ill,' he said. 'It's some kind of poison, but I don't know what it is.'

The two doctors looked around the room. There were two medicine bottles on a table: one said *Chloroform*, and the other *Laudanum*. Chloroform and laudanum were ordinary medicines. Many people in those days had them in their houses – they took them for headache or toothache. They weren't very dangerous; it would take an enormous amount of these medicines to kill somebody.

'He's not dying because of these medicines, is he?' said Dr Moore.

'No, I don't think so,' Dr Harrison agreed. 'He's far too ill for that.'

Florence Bravo was sitting on the bed beside her husband. She was washing his face with cool water.

'What's wrong with my husband, doctor?' she asked. 'He's not going to die, is he?'

Dr Moore put his hand on her arm. 'I'm sorry, Mrs Bravo,' he said. 'But your husband is really very ill. He has taken some terrible poison. He may not live long.'

Florence cried when he said that. She put her arms around her husband and kissed him. 'Oh, Charlie, please don't die!' she said. 'Come on, Charlie, you must get better. Speak to me – please don't leave me!'

But Charles was too ill to speak. The doctors gave him some medicine but it didn't help much. Florence watched, her face wet with tears. 'Charles's cousin is a doctor,' she said. 'Dr Royes Bell. He knows Charles very well – do you mind if I send for him?'

'No, that's all right,' Dr Harrison said. 'I'll write a letter for you.'

Dr Royes Bell knew Charles Bravo very well. He had met him in London that morning, and Charles had seemed happy and healthy as usual. He certainly said nothing about killing himself. So Dr Bell was very surprised when a letter from Dr Harrison arrived late that night.

Your cousin is very ill, the letter said. *Please come quickly; I think he is dying.*

Dr Royes Bell arrived at The Priory at about two o'clock in the morning. He brought with him another doctor, Dr George Johnson, who was both a friend and a well-known London doctor.

Charles was lying on his bed, asleep. His face was greyish white and he was breathing heavily. Dr Bell touched his face and his eyes opened.

'Charlie,' he said. 'Do you know who I am?'

For a moment Charles seemed not to understand, or recognize anybody around him. Then, after a minute, he said, 'Yes. You're Royes.'

'This is Dr Johnson,' Dr Bell said. 'We've come to help you, Charlie. How do you feel?'

'Terrible,' Charles answered. 'My stomach hurts. Let me out!' He suddenly jumped up and tried to get to the door, but the doctors held him and after a minute he fell back onto the bed. Dr Johnson gave him some medicine to take away the pain, and after a few minutes he began to look more comfortable.

Outside the room, the doctors spoke to Mrs Cox. 'You saw Mr Bravo first, before Dr Moore came,' Dr Johnson said. 'Did he say anything to you then?'

'Yes,' Mrs Cox answered. 'He said: "I've taken some of that poison; don't tell Florence."'

'Did he tell you what poison he took?'

'No,' Mrs Cox answered. 'Nothing more than that.'

When Dr Harrison heard this, he was angry. 'Why didn't you tell me that before?' he asked. 'You said he had taken chloroform, not poison.'

MR. ROYES BELL
DR. MOORE

DR. GEORGE JOHNSON
MR. GEORGE HARRISON

Four of the doctors who saw Charles Bravo before he died

The doctors went back into Charles's bedroom. 'Charlie, have you taken poison?' Dr Johnson asked.

'I rubbed my teeth with laudanum; perhaps I drank a little by mistake,' Charles replied.

'Laudanum wouldn't make you ill like this.'

'Well, if it isn't laudanum, I don't know what it is,' Charles said.

Then Florence came back in. There were tears on her face and she looked very tired. Charles held out his arms to her. 'Kiss me, my wife,' he said. Florence went to the bed and kissed him. Then she lay down beside him and touched his face gently with her fingers. The two doctors watched.

'What a lot of trouble I'm giving you, Florrie,' Charles said. 'Kiss me again. You've been the best of wives.'

'Oh, Charlie!' Florence said. 'What is the matter with you? What have you taken to make you so ill?'

Charles didn't answer. 'Oh, God help me!' he screamed in pain. Then he turned to his cousin and said: 'Royes, will I get better?'

'I hope so, Charlie, but you are very ill indeed.'

When Dr Bell said that, Charles looked frightened. 'Royes,' he said. 'Before I die, I want you to write something for me. Will you do that?'

Dr Bell wrote down Charles Bravo's words. *I leave everything I have to my wife, Florence Bravo.*

Charles sat up to write his name, and he and Dr Bell prayed to God together. Then he said: 'When I'm dead, Royes, look after Florence for me, will you? She's been the best of wives to me.'

At the Coroner's enquiry in July, some of the lawyers said that Florence killed her husband. But Charles's cousin, Dr Royes Bell, didn't believe that. Charles loved his wife, he told the lawyers. He left her everything. And Florence was very, very unhappy that night, when she saw her husband so ill. She called four doctors – Dr Moore, Dr Harrison, Dr Bell, and Dr Johnson. And on Thursday 20th April she sent for a *fifth* doctor, Dr William Gull.

Dr Gull was very famous and important, and was the doctor to Queen Victoria herself. He arrived at The Priory at six o'clock on Thursday evening. Charles Bravo was still alive, but he was very seriously ill.

'Mr Bravo, you have taken poison,' Dr Gull told him. 'Please tell me, who gave it to you?'

'I took it myself,' Charles Bravo said.

'What did you take?' Dr Gull asked.

'Laudanum,' Charles Bravo replied. 'I took some laudanum because I had toothache.'

'A little laudanum can't kill you, Mr Bravo,' Dr Gull said. 'What else did you take?'

'Nothing else. Only laudanum, doctor. That's all.'

'Mr Bravo, listen to me. You are very ill, you are going to die. It's important that you tell me the truth. What is this poison? If someone gave it to you, they wanted to kill you. Do you understand that?'

Charles Bravo shook his head slowly. 'It was only laudanum, doctor,' he said. 'No one gave it to me. I took it myself.'

That was the last thing he said to Dr Gull. A few hours later, Charles Bravo died. Five different doctors had seen him, and he told them all the same story. He had taken laudanum, he said, and then called for hot water to make himself sick.

'Where was he sick?' Dr Gull asked.

'Out of the window,' said Dr Johnson. 'Look, there.' He picked up some of the vomit from the roof with a silver spoon and put it in a glass bottle. Dr Gull sent it to Professor Redwood, a famous scientist, in London. Professor Redwood looked at it carefully.

'The poison was antimony,' the Professor told the Coroner later. 'I found ten grains of it in the vomit in the glass bottle. There were probably thirty grains in his body. That's what killed him.'

The antimony destroyed Charles Bravo's stomach. He died very slowly, in great pain.

But how did the antimony get into his stomach? That is the question. Antimony is a white powder. You can put very small amounts of it in a glass of wine, but it makes the wine look strange and taste awful. But if you put a lot of antimony in water, no one will notice. You can't see it or smell it or taste it. You can drink it like ordinary water. But a few minutes later, you will be very ill indeed.

Every evening, Charles Bravo drank from the bottle of water beside his bed. The antimony was probably in the bottle. But who put the antimony in the water? Charles Bravo, or someone else?

Dr Gull thought he knew. 'No one else killed Charles

Bravo,' he told Florence's father, Mr Campbell. 'Your daughter didn't kill him. He killed himself.'

But Charles's stepfather, Joseph Bravo, didn't agree. 'Charles was a strong, brave young man,' he said. 'He didn't kill himself. He was murdered.'

'Nonsense,' Florence's father said. 'Who wanted to kill him?'

'Ask your daughter,' Joseph Bravo said angrily. 'And her friends, Jane Cox and James Gully. One of them knows the answer, I'm sure.'

'I found ten grains of antimony.'

Chapter 11

The mystery

Did Charles Bravo kill himself, or was he murdered? After listening to everyone's story, the Coroner came to a decision.

THE TIMES

Friday 11th August 1876

Charles Bravo Murdered!

Yesterday the Coroner read out this decision: 'Mr Charles Bravo did not commit suicide and he did not die by accident. He was murdered with the poison antimony. But it is impossible to say which person – or persons – killed him.'

But was the Coroner right? And if so, who killed Charles Bravo? Over the years since 1876, many books and television programmes have asked these questions. But they have all given different answers.

The police learnt that the coachman, George Griffiths, was in Kent when Charles Bravo died, and his new employer said that was true. So Griffiths was not the murderer, but was he telling the truth when he said there was no antimony left in the stables? Perhaps there *was* some antimony left there – and someone found it, and used it. Or perhaps the antimony didn't come from the stables at all.

Here are the four main possible answers to the mystery.

First possible answer: Charles Bravo killed himself

It is difficult to believe that Charles Bravo *meant* to kill himself. Why would he do that? He was young and healthy, he seemed happy, he had a rich wife – he had every reason to live. And to die from antimony is a very painful, horrible death.

But perhaps he killed himself by accident. Is that possible? Think about it. Charles Bravo was not a very nice man. He married Florence for her money, not because he loved her. He hit her when she argued with him. She drank a lot of wine, and he didn't like that. Maybe he found the antimony in the stables, and put a little in her wine, to stop her drinking. After all, Florence did that to her first husband.

If he was using antimony in this way, perhaps he put some antimony in his water bottle by mistake; then forgot about it, and later drank from the bottle when he was thirsty.

Mrs Cox said he told her: 'I have taken *some of that* poison.' Did he really say that? And did Mrs Cox know which poison he was talking about? Probably not. She told Dr Harrison he had taken chloroform.

But then, if Charles knew he had taken antimony by

mistake, why didn't he tell the doctors about it? 'I only took laudanum, nothing else,' he told them. And laudanum didn't kill him.

Second possible answer: **Dr Gully killed Charles Bravo**

Dr Gully loved Florence. He wanted to marry her. He hated Charles Bravo, and he was worried and angry when Jane Cox told him that Charles sometimes hit Florence. Did Dr Gully write that letter to Charles Bravo saying: '*You don't love her. You only wanted her money, that's all.*'? Charles Bravo certainly thought so.

Dr Gully certainly wrote to Mrs Cox, and sent her medicine for her mother. He was a doctor, he could easily buy antimony if he wanted. And maybe he thought: 'If Charles Bravo is dead, then Florence will come back to me.'

But then, how could he get into the house, and into Charles Bravo's bedroom, to put the poison in the water bottle? No one saw him there; he hadn't been inside the house for months. But perhaps he *did* buy the antimony. And perhaps *another* person put it in the water bottle. Jane Cox, perhaps? Or Florence?

Dr Gully lived until 1882. The last years of his life were unhappy. No other doctors would speak to him or read his books. He didn't spend much time with Florence, either. She wasn't interested in him any more.

Third possible answer: **Jane Cox killed Charles Bravo**

Jane Cox was Florence's companion and her friend. She knew and liked Dr Gully but she thought he was too old for Florence. So she introduced her to a younger man, Charles Bravo.

At first she thought Charles was a good husband for Florence, but she soon changed her mind. He was angry and unkind; he hit Florence when she argued with him. He got rid of many servants, and he tried to get rid of Jane Cox, too. So Jane Cox would lose her friend, and her job. She had three sons at school – how would she pay for them?

Mrs Cox knew Charles Bravo drank from his water bottle every night. She could easily go into his bedroom and put antimony in the bottle.

There are many questions about Jane Cox.

Jane Cox answering questions at the Enquiry

When Charles opened his bedroom door, shouting for hot water, why didn't Mrs Cox come out? She wasn't asleep. But she did nothing until the maid, Mary Ann, came to fetch her. And then, when she went into Charles's bedroom, she sent Mary Ann out, again and again. Why? Because she wanted to be alone with Charles, perhaps? What did she do when she was alone with him? Give him more poison, perhaps? Burn the rest of the antimony on the fire? Clean out the water bottle, to make sure there were no grains of antimony left inside?

Why did she send for Dr Harrison, when Dr Moore lived much closer? Was she telling the truth, about what Charles said to her?

Some people say that Mrs Cox did it, because she was afraid of losing her job. She was a poor widow and needed the money.

But there is a problem with this, too. Jane Cox's aunt, who lived in Jamaica, was very rich. And her aunt was dying. A month *before* Charles Bravo died, this rich aunt had left all her money to Mrs Cox's son.

So Jane Cox didn't really need a job any more. And after Charles's death, she stopped working for Florence. She took her sons to Jamaica, and lived in a big house there. She was a rich lady, and died in 1917, aged ninety.

Perhaps she did kill Charles Bravo. But she didn't do it for the money.

Fourth possible answer: **Florence killed Charles Bravo**
Florence's first husband, Alexander Ricardo, died because

he drank too much. Before she left him, Florence tried to stop him drinking by putting small amounts of antimony in his wine, to make him sick.

Florence was a very rich young woman. She had a fine house, with lots of servants and horses. She liked to do things her own way. But she lived at a time when men told women what to do. When a man married a woman, all her money belonged to him. If a wife argued with her husband, the husband often hit her.

When Alexander hit her, Florence ran away, to Dr Gully. Dr Gully was the only man in her life who was kind to her. But she couldn't marry him, because he was too old and his wife was still alive. So she married Charles Bravo instead.

She was only married to Charles for five months. They had many arguments, and he often hit her. He sold her horses; he got rid of her coachman, George Griffiths. They argued about money, they argued about servants, they argued about her drinking. She lost her baby, and he tried to get rid of her friend, Jane Cox. Florence had many reasons to hate him.

Was she really asleep, when he drank the poison? Charles shouted for help outside her bedroom, but she didn't hear him. She lay in bed with her eyes closed.

Did she find some antimony in the stables? Did she put the antimony into his water bottle?

But then, when she woke up, she tried hard to save him. She sent for *five* different doctors. All the doctors thought she was very upset. And Charles didn't think she had killed him. 'You are the best of wives,' he said. His cousin, Dr Royes Bell, heard him. Charles left all his money to her.

After the enquiry, Florence Bravo left The Priory and went to live in Southsea, on the south coast of England. Her brother invited her to start a new life with him in Australia, but she refused. In Southsea she was lonely and unhappy. She didn't talk to Jane Cox or Dr Gully. She drank more and more wine every day. In September 1878, two years after her husband's death, she died. She had killed herself by drinking so much alcohol. She was thirty-three years old.

So did she love her husband, or did she kill him?

No one knows.

Charles and Florence Bravo

GLOSSARY

advertisement   a notice (e.g. in a newspaper) which tells people about jobs, things to sell, etc.

age   how old somebody is

alcohol   drinks like wine, beer, etc. that can make people drunk

amount   how much there is of something

antimony   a poisonous chemical used in the past as a medicine

behave   to do and say things in a certain way

believe   to think that something is true or right

breathe   to take in or send out air through your nose and mouth

bruise   a dark mark on the skin that comes after something hits it

camphor   a chemical with a strong smell, used in medicine

carriage   a vehicle, pulled by horses, used for carrying people

chest   the front part of the top of the body

chloroform   a strong chemical used in the past in medicine

coach   a large closed vehicle, pulled by horses, used in the past for carrying people; coachman a man who drives a coach

companion   a person (often a woman) whose job is to live with and help somebody

congratulations   said to someone when you are happy about their good luck or success

coroner   a person whose job is to discover the cause of any sudden or suspicious death

cousin   the child of your uncle or aunt

damn   a swear word that people use to show they are angry

darling   a name that you call somebody that you love

drunk *(adj)*   having drunk too much alcohol and behaving badly

enormous   very big

enquiry   an official meeting to find out the truth about something

expect   to think or believe that something will happen

fault if something bad is your fault, you made it happen
get rid of to make yourself free of somebody or something that
   you do not want
grain a very, very small amount of some medicines
groom a person whose job is to look after horses
guardian a person who is responsible in law for somebody else,
   e.g. a child or (at the time of this story) a woman
handsome good-looking (usually of a boy or man)
handwriting the way you write
horrible very bad, terrible; making you very afraid or unhappy
kiss to touch someone lovingly with your lips
kneel (past tense **knelt**) to bend your legs and put your knees on
   the ground
laudanum a drug used in the past to make people feel happy
law all the rules of a country
lawyer someone whose job is helping people with the law
maid (**maidservant**) a female servant in a house
marriage the legal relationship between a husband and wife
mustard a thick yellow sauce, eaten cold with meat (used in the
   past as a medicine)
normal usual, ordinary
ordinary usual; not special or different in any way
perfect as good as it can possibly be
pleasure a strong feeling of enjoyment
poison something that can kill you or make you very ill if you
   eat or drink it
powder a dry mixture of very small pieces
pray to talk to God
pregnant expecting a baby
rub to move something backwards and forwards on another
   thing
servant someone who works in another person's house

stable a building where horses are kept; stable yard a flat hard piece of land outside a stable

stepfather a man who has married your mother but is not your father

suicide the act of killing yourself

sweat water that comes from your skin when you are hot or afraid

tears water that comes from the eyes when you cry

truth the facts; what is true, what really happened

upset unhappy or worried

vomit *(v & n)* to bring food from the stomach back out through the mouth

widow a woman whose husband has died

wine an alcoholic drink made from grapes

ACTIVITIES

Before Reading

1 **Read the story introduction on the first page of the book, and the back cover. How much do you know now about the story? Choose T (True) or NT (Not True) for each sentence.**

    1 In Queen Victoria's time, husbands could tell their wives what to do.

    2 Florence's lover was nicer to her than her first husband was.

    3 The doctors did not know what killed Charles Bravo.

    4 Everybody knew who had killed Charles Bravo.

    5 Florence met Dr Gully before she married Charles Bravo.

    6 Nobody had any reason for wanting to kill Charles Bravo.

2 **Do you agree (A), slightly disagree (S), or strongly disagree (D) with these ideas?**

    1 Women should leave their husbands if they are cruel.

    2 It is right for women to obey their husbands in everything.

    3 If it is all right for a husband to beat a wife, then it must also be all right for a wife to beat a husband.

    4 If a husband is not kind to his wife, she should ask her friends to help her.

    5 It is always wrong to murder somebody.

    6 If you love somebody, it doesn't matter if you are married to them or not.

ACTIVITIES

While Reading

As you read this book, and the different stories told by Florence Bravo, Dr Gully, and Jane Cox, stop at the places listed below. Before you read on, think about the big question in this story.

Read Chapters 1 to 3, and then think about this . . .

- Who killed Charles Bravo? What do you think at this point in the story?

Read Chapters 4 and 5, and then think about this . . .

- Who killed Charles Bravo? Has your opinion changed? Why, or why not?

Read Chapters 6 and 7, and then think about this . . .

- Who killed Charles Bravo? Are you more sure, or less sure, than before? Did more than one person do it? If yes, which people did it?

Read Chapter 8, and then think about this . . .

- Who killed Charles Bravo? What has changed now? Is there anything suspicious in Florence's story?

Read Chapter 9, and then think about this . . .

- Who killed Charles Bravo? Do you expect to learn anything new from the doctors, or have you made up your mind? Who is the most probable killer, and who is the least probable killer, in your opinion?

ACTIVITIES

After Reading

1 So who killed Charles Bravo? Was it murder, or did he kill himself by accident? What do *you* think? Write three or four sentences to explain your ideas.

2 Fill in the gaps with names, and match the parts of sentences together. Then choose the best linking words to join them.

Charles Bravo / Florence Bravo / Jane Cox / Dr Gully /
Mary Anne Keeber / Alexander Ricardo

1 _____ wanted to marry Florence . . .

2 _____ did not want to leave her job . . .

3 _____ wanted Florence's money for himself . . .

4 _____ started drinking a lot . . .

5 _____ put the bottle of drinking water in Charles Bravo's room every night . . .

6 _____ thought that at last she had found the perfect husband . . .

7 *when / because* she thought Charles would hit Florence again.

8 *but / so* she had no reason to kill him.

9 *when / until* she met Charles Bravo.

10 *because / but* he had a wife already.

11 *after / so* he left the army.

12 *and / so* he got rid of three horses and two gardeners.

3 **Perhaps this is what some of the other characters in this story think about the Bravos. Which characters are they?**

1 'I wasn't sad when I heard the news. I liked working for her, because she cared about the horses. But him! He only cared about money, and he didn't listen to anybody. I didn't kill him, but I'm not surprised that he's dead . . .'

2 'I was halfway down the stairs when Mr Bravo opened his door and started shouting for hot water. Why didn't Mrs Bravo or Mrs Cox hear him? He shouted loudly enough. I think it's very strange that they didn't hear him . . .'

3 'I liked working at The Priory. Mrs Ricardo was a beautiful, kind lady, and she liked to talk about the flowers in her garden, and about my family. And then suddenly, after the wedding, I had to look for a new job. Well, it's the husband's job to decide about these things. But I know this – she was happier before she married him . . .'

4 'Something very strange happened, I'm sure of that. He was a healthy young man when he lived with us, and I liked him very much. He was like a son to me. Why did he die? I think Florence knows something about it. She's lost two husbands – that's not good. Perhaps Jane Cox helped her. I don't think he killed himself – and his mother doesn't think so either . . .'

5 'He was happy and well when I saw him earlier that day. He wasn't thinking about suicide. I'm sure that he loved Florence – he called her 'the best of wives'. Those were his actual words to me that night. And she loved him too . . .'

4 There are 20 words from the story in this word search. Find the words (they go from left to right, and from top to bottom) and draw lines through them. The words are 4 letters or longer, and there is one plural noun.

B	R	E	A	T	H	E	U	P	S	E	T
R	H	X	I	E	F	A	U	L	T	S	D
U	C	P	R	A	Y	E	C	H	E	S	T
I	O	E	A	R	T	H	W	I	N	E	S
S	R	C	S	S	E	R	V	A	N	T	U
E	O	T	W	W	I	D	O	W	W	A	I
S	N	A	E	N	O	R	M	O	U	S	C
B	E	H	A	V	E	N	I	A	C	C	I
T	R	U	T	H	I	D	T	E	N	T	D
K	I	S	S	P	E	R	F	E	C	T	E

Now look at the word search again, and write down all the letters without a line through them. Begin with the first line, and go across each line to the end. You should have 21 letters, which will make a sentence of 5 words.

1 What is the hidden sentence?
2 Do you agree with it? Explain why you agree, or don't agree.

5 Imagine that Florence was tried for murder. Here are two speeches by the lawyers; the first says that Florence did murder Charles, the second says that she did not. Choose one suitable word to fill each gap. Which lawyer do you believe?

1 'Florence Bravo is a _____. She thought that Charles would be the _____ husband. But when she _____ out that she

was _____, she decided to kill him. She had used _____
before, when she tried to stop her _____ husband from
drinking. And she was friendly with her _____, George
Griffiths, who _____ antimony in the stables. Of _____ she
sent for a lot of doctors. She _____ everybody to think that
she _____ Charles and wanted him to live. But really she
wanted to get _____ of him.'

2 '_____ would Florence kill Charles? He was young and
handsome, and she _____ being with him. Of course they
_____ sometimes – but lots of husbands and _____ argue,
and they don't kill _____ other! Florence got upset easily,
that's all. Florence wanted to have _____, and she could
not do that _____ Charles. Other _____ hated Charles, and
it is not difficult to get antimony. No, Charles _____ she
was the _____ of wives, and he was right.'

6 **What did you think about the people in this story? Fill in names
where needed, and complete these sentences in your own
words.**

1 I felt sorry for _____ because _____.
2 I think _____ was the luckiest person because _____.
3 I think _____ was right to _____.
4 I think _____ was wrong to _____.
5 I liked _____ because _____.
6 I didn't like _____ because _____.
7 I think the strangest part of the story is when _____.

ABOUT THE AUTHOR

Tim Vicary was born in London in 1949. He attended Cambridge University and then worked as a schoolteacher, and is now a teaching fellow at the Norwegian Study Centre at the University of York. He is married, has two children, and lives in the country in Yorkshire, in the north of England. He has written coursebooks for use in Norwegian secondary schools, and has also published two historical novels, *The Blood Upon the Rose*, and *Cat and Mouse*, under his own name, and a crime novel, *A Game of Proof*, under the pseudonym Megan Stark. His website is www.timvicary.com.

He has written nearly twenty books for Oxford Bookworms. Some of his other titles at Stage 3 are *Chemical Secret*, *Justice*, and *The Brontë Story*. Other True Stories include *Grace Darling*, *The Elephant Man*, and *Mutiny on the Bounty*.

The mystery of Charles Bravo is one of the great unsolved crimes of British legal history, and Tim has been interested in it for many years. Sometimes he thinks that perhaps Dr Gully and Jane Cox did it together: Dr Gully gave Jane the poison and Mrs Cox put it in Charles Bravo's water jug. But Dr Gully was such a decent, honest man, not like a murderer at all. And of course, the person who had the best reason to want to kill Charles Bravo was his wife, Florence. All the questions come back to her.

The problem is that there is not enough evidence. Perhaps one day a modern detective, with all the forensic skills of today, will be able to go back in time to investigate this story when all the people (except Charles Bravo) were still alive. That would be a very interesting story!

OXFORD BOOKWORMS LIBRARY

Classics • Crime & Mystery • Factfiles • Fantasy & Horror
Human Interest • Playscripts • Thriller & Adventure
True Stories • World Stories

The OXFORD BOOKWORMS LIBRARY provides enjoyable reading in English, with a wide range of classic and modern fiction, non-fiction, and plays. It includes original and adapted texts in seven carefully graded language stages, which take learners from beginner to advanced level. An overview is given on the next pages.

All Stage 1 titles are available as audio recordings, as well as over eighty other titles from Starter to Stage 6. All Starters and many titles at Stages 1 to 4 are specially recommended for younger learners. Every Bookworm is illustrated, and Starters and Factfiles have full-colour illustrations.

The OXFORD BOOKWORMS LIBRARY also offers extensive support. Each book contains an introduction to the story, notes about the author, a glossary, and activities. Additional resources include tests and worksheets, and answers for these and for the activities in the books. There is advice on running a class library, using audio recordings, and the many ways of using Oxford Bookworms in reading programmes. Resource materials are available on the website <www.oup.com/bookworms>.

The *Oxford Bookworms Collection* is a series for advanced learners. It consists of volumes of short stories by well-known authors, both classic and modern. Texts are not abridged or adapted in any way, but carefully selected to be accessible to the advanced student.

You can find details and a full list of titles in the *Oxford Bookworms Library Catalogue* and *Oxford English Language Teaching Catalogues*, and on the website <www.oup.com/bookworms>.

THE OXFORD BOOKWORMS LIBRARY
GRADING AND SAMPLE EXTRACTS

STARTER • 250 HEADWORDS

present simple – present continuous – imperative –
can/cannot, must – *going to* (future) – simple gerunds …

Her phone is ringing – but where is it?

Sally gets out of bed and looks in her bag. No phone. She looks under the bed. No phone. Then she looks behind the door. There is her phone. Sally picks up her phone and answers it. *Sally's Phone*

STAGE 1 • 400 HEADWORDS

… past simple – coordination with *and, but, or* –
subordination with *before, after, when, because, so* …

I knew him in Persia. He was a famous builder and I worked with him there. For a time I was his friend, but not for long. When he came to Paris, I came after him – I wanted to watch him. He was a very clever, very dangerous man. *The Phantom of the Opera*

STAGE 2 • 700 HEADWORDS

… present perfect – *will* (future) – (*don't*) *have to, must not, could* –
comparison of adjectives – simple *if* clauses – past continuous –
tag questions – *ask/tell* + infinitive …

While I was writing these words in my diary, I decided what to do. I must try to escape. I shall try to get down the wall outside. The window is high above the ground, but I have to try. I shall take some of the gold with me – if I escape, perhaps it will be helpful later. *Dracula*

STAGE 3 • 1000 HEADWORDS

... should, may – present perfect continuous – *used to* – past perfect –
causative – relative clauses – indirect statements ...

Of course, it was most important that no one should see
Colin, Mary, or Dickon entering the secret garden. So Colin
gave orders to the gardeners that they must all keep away
from that part of the garden in future. *The Secret Garden*

STAGE 4 • 1400 HEADWORDS

... past perfect continuous – passive (simple forms) –
would conditional clauses – indirect questions –
relatives with *where/when* – gerunds after prepositions/phrases ...

I was glad. Now Hyde could not show his face to the world
again. If he did, every honest man in London would be
proud to report him to the police. *Dr Jekyll and Mr Hyde*

STAGE 5 • 1800 HEADWORDS

... future continuous – future perfect –
passive (modals, continuous forms) –
would have conditional clauses – modals + perfect infinitive ...

If he had spoken Estella's name, I would have hit him. I was
so angry with him, and so depressed about my future, that I
could not eat the breakfast. Instead I went straight to the old
house. *Great Expectations*

STAGE 6 • 2500 HEADWORDS

... passive (infinitives, gerunds) – advanced modal meanings –
clauses of concession, condition

When I stepped up to the piano, I was confident. It was as if
I knew that the prodigy side of me really did exist. And when I
started to play, I was so caught up in how lovely I looked that I
didn't worry how I would sound. *The Joy Luck Club*

BOOKWORMS · TRUE STORIES · STAGE 3

The Brontë Story

TIM VICARY

On a September day in 1821, in the church of a Yorkshire village, a man and six children stood around a grave. They were burying a woman: the man's wife, the children's mother. The children were all very young, and within a few years the two oldest were dead, too.

Close to the wild beauty of the Yorkshire moors, the father brought up his young family. Who had heard of the Brontës of Haworth then? Branwell died while he was still a young man, but the three sisters who were left had an extraordinary gift. They could write marvellous stories – *Jane Eyre*, *Wuthering Heights*, *The Tenant of Wildfell Hall* . . . But Charlotte, Emily, and Anne Brontë did not live to grow old or to enjoy their fame. Only their father was left, alone with his memories.

BOOKWORMS · TRUE STORIES · STAGE 3

Rabbit-Proof Fence

DORIS PILKINGTON GARIMARA

Retold by Jennifer Bassett

Fourteen-year-old Molly and her cousins Daisy and Gracie were mixed-race Aborigines. In 1931 they were taken away from their families and sent to a camp to be trained as good 'white' Australians. They were told to forget their mothers, their language, their home.

But Molly would not forget. She and her cousins escaped and walked back to Jigalong, 1600 kilometres away, following the rabbit-proof fence north across Western Australia to their desert home.

Rabbit-Proof Fence is the true story of that walk, told by Molly's daughter, Doris. It is also a prize-winning film.